Why Not Now?

By Denise Leduc
Illustrated by Karin Sköld

Why Not Now? by Denise Leduc

© 2022 Denise Leduc
ISBN: 978-1-7782869-3-3

All Rights Reserved. No part of this publication may be reproduced, distributed, or transmitted in any form or by any means, or stored in a database or retrieval system, without the prior written permission of the publisher, except as permitted under the Canadian Copyright Act.

This is a work of fiction. All people, places, and incidents are products of the authors imagination. Any resemblances to people, living or dead, or any incidents is coincidental.

Illustrations by Karin Sköld
www.karinskold.com

Published by Lilac Arch Press
Saskatchewan, Canada
www.lilacarchpress.com

Dedicated to my father
who taught me
"Why Not Now?"

Table of Contents

Chapter 1–page 7

Chapter 2–page 13

Chapter 3–page 20

Chapter 4–page 27

Chapter 5–page 34

Chapter 6–page 37

Chapter 7–page 46

Chapter 8–page 53

Chapter 9–page 59

Chapter 10–page 66

Chapter 1

Arriving at the Vancouver airport, Frank felt reinvigorated. It had been a long time since he had been on an airplane. He was glad his son, John, had insisted on him coming.

They weaved their way through the crowd of travelers looking for his grandson, Max.

"There he is," said John.

Frank hardly recognized him. He still pictured Max as that kid with big blue eyes who loved to swim. Frank was now looking at a grown man.

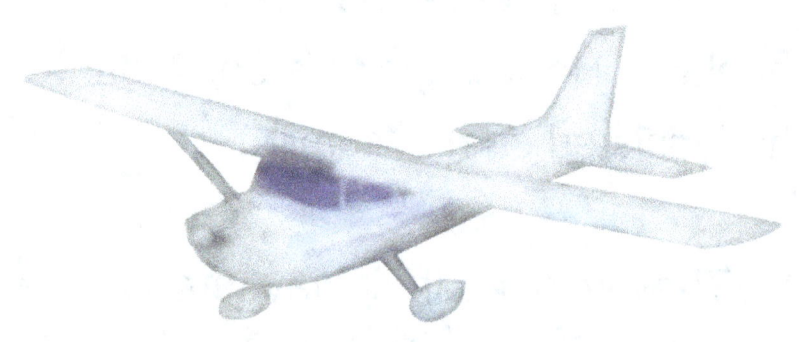

"Hey there, Gramps," said Max pulling Frank into a strong bear hug. "I'm so happy you came. We are going to have a great time."

Frank thought about how much time he had spent with Max as a child. He had taught the boy to bait a hook, sail a boat, and somersault off the diving board. He had also taken Max on his first scuba dive.

Living on the shores of Lake Huron meant the family's life had been all about the water.

But time marched on. Frank certainly wasn't doing somersaults off the diving board anymore. Max had grown and set out for his own adventures. Now, he was a helicopter pilot out here in the mountains.

Frank was proud of all his grandchildren, but there was something special about Max. Max reminded him of his younger self and what might have been.

Life had been good for Frank. His father had secured him a good job down at the factory. He had married a good woman. They'd had some great kids and a lovely home.

Yet, from time to time, Frank wondered. What would life have been like if he'd ventured away from his hometown? What if he had taken a couple more risks? What if he'd been a little more like Max?

There was no sense thinking about all that now. Life had been good to him, and he had no regrets. Maybe though, if he was a little bit younger, he'd be able to have one more adventure.

Frank followed his son and his grandson out to Max's truck.

Chapter 1 Discussion Questions

1. Have you ever been on an airplane?

_____

2. Where are the places you have traveled to?

_____

_____

3. Did you stay in your hometown or move away?

_____

4. Do you have family and friends in different parts of the country or world?

_____

_____

5. Are there any outdoor activities you've enjoyed?

Chapter 2

Frank did not envy the traffic of Vancouver. On the contrary, he was grateful he was not the one driving. Max seemed natural as he maneuvered his way through the busy city.

Their first stop was Stanley Park. First, Frank marveled at the giant trees. Then, he delighted on the beach, dipping his hand in the Pacific Ocean.

"Well, that's a first," he smiled.

As they were getting back in the truck, Max asked, "So, what do you want to do on your ten days in B.C., Gramps?"

"Oh, I don't know. I came to see you. Whatever you guys want to do is fine with me."

"Dad comes out here all the time, and I live here. This is your first time here. It's all about you."

"Well, it's May, so I guess skiing is out," joked Frank.

"Actually, there's still snow on the mountains. Do you want to go skiing, Gramps?"

"At my age? Not a chance."
"I don't know," John chimed in, "You still might have what it takes."
"Nope," Frank stated firmly.

Frank thought about what he wanted to do while he was here. His only goal had been to visit with Max. He'd seen many photos, but he wanted to see Max's home, meet his fiancée, Tara, and witness the life he had created.

When Frank spoke up, Max and John had been discussing the pros and cons of getting a new truck. "You know," he said, "I always love seeing your photography. Could we go to some places where you get those great shots?"

"You bet," said Max. "I know some perfect spots."

Frank loved that the highway they traveled on was called the Sea-to-Sky Highway. The name was beautiful, and the scenery did not disappoint.

"My home is about a hundred miles from here," Max shared. "I live a bit north of Whistler."

Frank had heard of Whistler, but he had never been there. The mountains and Whistler were what first lured Max here across the country.

"We can check out Whistler one of the days, Gramps," Max suggested. "We can ride the gondola and go for lunch."

"Or you might change your mind and try the skiing," John teased.

As they traveled further from the city, Frank saw this was Max's natural habitat. He seemed at home as he drove this highway. From time to time, Max would even venture off the main highway to show them an exciting spot. A couple of times, they even spotted a bear.

"What do you think, Gramps?"

"I think you live in paradise," Frank answered.

Chapter 2 Discussion Questions

1. Do you prefer city living or country living?
___

2. Have you ever dipped your hand in or swam in the ocean?
___

3. Have you ever been skiing or done any other winter sports?
___

4. What is the prettiest place you have lived or visited?
___

5. What are some memories of younger people in your life?
___
___
___

Chapter 3

Frank could have spent all day driving this highway. Though tired from a day of excitement, he wasn't quite ready for the journey to be over.

As they pulled into the small town Max called home, Frank took a moment to let it all sink in. So this was where his youngest grandchild had made a home for himself.

Imagine, he thought, waking up every morning surrounded by these mountains, by this big sky. Max parked the truck in front of a green bungalow.

As he stepped out of the truck, Frank took a deep breath of the mountain air.

"Welcome to my place," said Max.

Max opened the door, and a dog bounded out, greeting his favorite human. The dog soon made his way to revisit his old friend John. Finally, the dog introduced himself to Frank.

"I see Jake likes you," said Max.

Inside, Max fed the dog, then showed his grandfather around. The home was simple and modern. Max went for understated home decor.

The garage and the yard were another story, though. That was where Max kept all his toys. Max seemed to have the gear for everything from winter to water sports.

He also had started a vegetable garden in the backyard.

"This was Tara's idea," Max admitted. "I can't wait for you to meet her."

"And you met her at work? She's a pilot too?"

"Yes, I am," came a female voice.

The men turned around. A cute brunette with a smiling face greeted them.

"Tara, I want you to meet my grandpa."

"Hello, Mr.," Tara started.

Frank cut her off, "Just Frank. Please call me Frank."

"Okay, Frank. It is a pleasure to meet you. Max has told me so much about you."

"All good, I hope."

Tara took Frank's hand. "May I show you my plans for the garden?"

As they toured the garden, Tara shared, "I know Max isn't the most expressive guy. But I hope you know how much Max adores you."

Frank had never thought about it. "Really?" he asked.

Tara nodded.

She shared, "He says you're his hero. He's always looked up to you."

Frank had never been called anyone's hero before.

Tara giggled, "And the stories he tells me. You sure made his childhood fun."

They sat down on the garden swing.

"Truth is," said Frank, "Max always made my life fun too."

"Max and I have discussed the desire to have children," Tara confided. "I know we live far away, but I sure do hope I can count on you to add some fun to the lives of any little ones that might come along."

Chapter 3 Discussion Questions

1. How would you describe the place you live? What is your style?
_____

2. Do you/or have you had any pets?
_____

3. What are some memories of older generations in your family?
_____
_____

4. Grandparents can be more fun than parents. Is there something fun you remember about your grandparents? Is there something fun you remember about grandchildren in your life?
_____
_____

Chapter 4

Max suggested they go for a drive the next day, and he could show Frank some of his favorite spots.

Their first stop was a nearby river.

"You should see the fishing here," Max gushed. "The salmon can be over 50 lbs."

Frank had never fished for salmon, though he did enjoy eating it.

"There is nothing quite like fresh salmon," Max shared.

"We should come back tomorrow and do some fishing," John suggested.

They all agreed that sounded like a good plan.

Max asked as they left the river area, "Can I show you two something?"

"Of course," said John. "What do you think, Dad?"

"Sounds good to me," answered Frank.

Max turned in a new direction. It didn't take long before they were in a densely wooded area. The paved road had ended, and they were on some type of extensive trail.

"These are old logging roads," Max explained.

The path was steep, but Max knew what he was doing. So higher and higher they climbed in the pick-up truck.

"There's a little property that has come up for sale," Max said. "It's a beautiful lot. We think it might be the perfect spot for Tara and me to build a home together."

Frank's ears perked up. Indeed, Max wouldn't want to drive up this mountain every day.

Before he could ask, Max explained further, "There is a ledge up here where we can park. Then, we can get a fantastic overhead view of the property."

"That's quite something," Frank said. But, of course, it wasn't every day one could get an aerial view of some real estate.

"We're almost there," Max said.

Frank was sure they'd been climbing up the mountain a half hour or more. They were going slow, but Frank wondered what altitude they might be.

The logging road opened to a clearing, and Max made his way to park. Expecting to be the only ones here, they were all surprised by what they saw.

Chapter 4 Discussion Questions

1. Have you ever enjoyed fishing?
_____

2. Do you like eating fish? If so, what kinds?
_____
_____

3. Have you ever visited the mountains?
_____

4. Using your imagination, what might they have seen that surprised them?
_____
_____
_____
_____

Chapter 5

The clearing where Max parked was dotted with other vehicles that had made the trek up the mountain.

Several people were also sitting on blankets on the side of the mountain.

"I've never seen anything like this," Max admitted. "Usually, it's only me and the wildlife up here."

The three men gravitated towards the groups of people hanging out on the blankets. Was there an event here today? Was it an organization having a picnic?

Frank saw some young fellows with open cans of beer. Maybe, it was a place for young people to escape and hang out.

"Wow," said John, "Look at that."

Frank looked around but didn't see what his son was referring to.

"No, Dad," said John, "Look up."
Frank looked up. He was not expecting this.

Chapter 5 Discussion Questions

1. Why do you think the folks were hanging out on the side of the mountain?

_____

_____

2. What do you think they saw when they looked up?

_____

_____

Chapter 6

Half a dozen people were gliding over the trees in the air. They were tethered to brightly colored canopies. The folks on the ground seemed to be there with the paragliders.

"That is awesome," commented Max.

"It sure is," agreed John.

Frank thought it was impressive too. Oh, to be young again.

One paraglider came in for a landing.

"I've got to go over and chat with him," said John. "I'd love to learn more about what they're doing."

Max showed Frank the property that had been the intention for their trip up the mountain. It was a beautiful piece of land. Frank could imagine Max and Tara building a home there. It would be an idyllic place to raise the future children Tara had expressed hope for.

John was still talking to the paraglider when Frank and Max decided to take a large rock as a resting place.

"Have you ever done anything like that," Frank asked his grandson, motioning to the people still in the sky.

"Me? No way. I'm scared of heights."

"Scared of heights?" Frank replied. "How can a pilot have a fear of heights?"

"It's different, Gramps," Max explained. "The machine makes all the difference."

They both watched as the people continued to glide over the landscape.

"Up there," Max continued, "It's just you and not much else."

Frank conceded to that. Still, there was something spectacular about it.

Frank thought for a moment. "You ski," he said. "When you start at the top of the mountain, that's high up."

"Nope, different," said Max. "My feet always stay on the ground." Then, he chuckled, "Well, I should say, they usually stay on the ground."

Frank smiled.

John approached them. He was beaming.

"Those guys are amazing. That looks like so much fun. He offered to take me up."

"What?"

"Yeah, they can strap a passenger to them. They do all the work, but you get the experience. Isn't that great?"

"Are you going to do it, Dad?" Max asked.

"Not today," John answered. "I have to work up the nerve. I need to work on my fear of heights."

There was silence for a moment as each man watched the paragliding some more.

"But, one day," John continued, " I will do it. I even took the fellow's phone number for the day I am ready."

"Nope, no way," said Max. "I can say I won't be trying that."

In a quiet voice, Frank said, "I'd do it."

"Really, Gramps?" Max's blue eyes grew wide.

"So, do it!" encouraged John.

Shocked, Frank replied, "What? Right now?"

"Why not now?" answered John. "You're here. He's here willing to take someone up. The weather is ideal. You couldn't ask for a more perfect day. Why not now?"

Because I am too old, thought Frank. Because I have never done anything so spontaneous. Because I don't know what I am doing. Because I don't know if I am dressed right for such an activity. Because the idea is ridiculous.

But then, Frank took a deep breath, looked over the mountain ledge and into the sky, and reflected on those words. Why not now?

Chapter 6 Discussion Questions

1. Have you ever done an activity such as paragliding?

---

2. Max and John have a fear of heights. This is a common fear. Is there anything you have a fear of?

---

3. Do you think Frank will try paragliding?

---

4. Do you think Frank should try paragliding? Why or why not?

Chapter 7

"Okay," said Frank.
"Okay? asked Max.
"Okay," asserted Frank.

"Yes!" cheered Max doing a celebratory jump.

"Okay," confirmed John. "Let me talk to the guy again before he heads out solo."
John was so excited he almost seemed to gallop to the paraglider.

Looking at Max, Frank asked, "What did I agree to?"

Max grinned, "To some adventure."

"Yeah," Frank reflected, "I forgot I might be a little too old for adventure."

"You got this, Gramps," Max assured.

John came back over. "It's all set up," he said. "He's going to take you up."

"He wasn't concerned about my age?"

"No."

"Did you tell him I've never done this before?"

"Go on," encouraged John. "We're burning daylight."

John took Frank over to the paraglider. Frank shook his hand.

"So, with these straps, I am going to attach you to me," he said. He continued showing Frank the gear they would use and gave him an overview of what they would do.

"I have a radio with me at all times. If the wind carries us away, it's no problem. I'll radio my friend here," he said, nodding towards another fellow. "Then he will hop in his truck and come get us."

Landing, Frank hadn't thought about that. How were they going to land? Never mind the landing; how were they going to take off?

"How do we get in the air? Frank questioned.

The fellow pointed to the edge of the mountain twenty feet ahead.

"We run," he said. "We run off the side of the mountain."

Run off the mountain. The thought was so incredible Frank had to laugh out loud.

Soon, I will be flying like an eagle, Frank mused to himself. He looked around this place. Perched atop a nearby tree, an eagle seemed to be watching him. Frank winked at the serious-looking bird.

"So, for the landing, do we just run back onto the mountain?" Frank queried.

"Pretty much," the fellow answered with a straight face.

Oh heavens, thought Frank. What have I gotten myself into?

Chapter 7 Discussion Questions

1. What is something spontaneous you have done?

_____

_____

2. What do you think about what Frank is about to do?

_____

_____

Chapter 8

It didn't seem long before Frank was wearing a helmet and strapped to a stranger.

The fellow said, "In a moment, we're going to start a slow jog. All you have to do is keep moving your feet. Once we leave the ground, the wind and our wing above will do most of the work. I will steer us. You can hang out and enjoy the view."

Max was close by, still cheering his grandfather on. "You'll be great, Gramps. I'll take a video on my phone. You'll be able to show everyone back home."

Before he knew it the fellow gave the word and Frank was doing it. He was actually running off the side of the mountain!

As his feet left the ground he thought, oh gosh, what if I die?

The thought was fleeting. Soon, the wind carried them higher and higher. He looked down to see Max and John waving at him. He saw the tops of trees. He saw the valley below.

Well, if it's my time to go, Frank thought, so be it. This is too amazing to miss.

To his left, he spotted an eagle in flight. Was it the same eagle he had seen earlier? As he looked down at the trees he thought how he truly did have a bird's eye view.

After that initial rush of adrenaline, Frank began to relax. It was peaceful up here. He took in the mountains beside him, the sky around him, the trees below, and the occasional bird. He felt connected to all of nature around him.

I could get used to this, he thought. John had been right. The weather was exactly right. It was a perfect day for this. Frank was thankful he had taken the risk.

The experience both felt like it was over in a heartbeat and seemed to go on forever. Frank was wearing a watch.

Yet, though he had relaxed as he glided through the sky, he didn't dare move around too much. His hands had been holding onto some straps this whole time. He knew it was silly. Holding onto them provided no real benefit. But they did offer him a sense of security. He didn't want to move his hand to check the time.

So, there he was—amongst nature, at peace, in this timeless state. This was perfection. This was bliss.

Chapter 8 Discussion Questions

1. It used to be to make a video, folks needed expensive equipment. Now, anyone with a cell phone can make a video. So, what are some things you love about technology?

_____
_____

2. Are there any places in nature that bring you a feeling of peace?

_____
_____

3. When was a time you took a risk, and it was worth it?

_____
_____
_____

Chapter 9

The landing back onto the ground was less than graceful for all the perfection of being in the air. After an indeterminate amount of time, Frank's guide began steering them back. Though they had journeyed far from the mountain, the wind worked with them. They had no problem returning to where they had started. Hence, they did not need to radio for a truck to pick them up at a distant spot.

As they approached the mountain, John and Max came into view. Max was hooting and hollering as he held his phone high to capture Frank's image.

They got closer, and Frank started moving his legs, trying to run back onto the mountain. At first, it seemed as though he would be successful.

One foot touched the earth, then the other. Left, then right as they tried to reestablish firm contact with solid ground.

But then Frank's feet couldn't quite keep up. So, to his embarrassment, he took a little tumble. Quickly though, he was able to get himself up and brush himself off.

"Are you okay?" the paraglider asked.

"I'm okay. No doubt, I looked a little clumsy, though."

"It's all good. You did great. Those landings take some practice," the fellow assured him.

Max and John were over right away.

"Woo-hoo!" Max exclaimed. "That was brilliant. You looked fantastic up there."

"It was so awesome watching you up there," John agreed.

"Gramps, you are the coolest guy I know."

They all took turns shaking the paraglider's hand.

"Next time," John promised, "I will go for it."

Max went back to the large rock and sat down.

"Gramps, can I post this video on YouTube? I can make it private, then send the link to all the relatives so they can see what you have been up to your first full day in B.C."

"Oh, son," John said, "You should leave it public, then anyone can watch. He'll be an inspiration, a YouTube sensation.

"As long as you cut that landing out, I don't care what you do with it," Frank said, grinning.

"Sure thing," said Max. "Give me a couple of minutes to do some quick edits."

After he had finished, Max asked, "Are you sure it's okay with you if it's public? Anyone would be able to see. But Dad's right; it will be inspiring."

Frank shrugged as he looked out over the vast mountains, "Do whatever you want with it. After today's adventure, I'm up for anything."

Chapter 9 Discussion Questions

1. Frank fell, but he got back up. What is a time in your life you persevered through a challenge?

_____

_____

_____

2. Have you ever checked out videos on YouTube? If you have, what kind of videos do you enjoy?

_____

3. What are things you look to for inspiration?

_____

_____

4. Who has been someone inspiring in your life?

_____

Chapter 10

It wasn't until they descended the mountain that Frank finally started to come back to earth. Even though his body had landed, his head still felt like it had been in the clouds for quite a while.

Excited, Max and John were chatting in the front seat. Frank was quiet and reflective in the backseat. Had he done what he'd just done? He thought he should pinch himself to see if it had all been a dream. But, he knew this adventure had been real.

"This was only day one of your visit," Max said, "I can't wait to see how you're going to top this tomorrow."

Frank didn't think anything could ever top this experience. It was the thrill of a lifetime.

"You know," Frank mused, "I was up there with the birds tethered to a stranger, and I didn't even catch the fellow's name."

Tara was waiting on the front porch when they arrived back at Max's place. She jumped up and ran to give Frank a big hug as soon as he had exited the truck.

"I saw the video," she gushed. "Spectacular! You were so awesome. I want to hear all about it."

Frank appreciated her enthusiasm.

Yet, he wasn't quite sure if he had all the words to express the exhilaration he had felt while he sailed through the sky.

Tara was still chattering joyfully. "I brought pizza for the daredevil," she said. "I hear bacon, ham, and mushroom is your favorite.

Frank beamed, "I hope the whole pizza is for me. I have never been so hungry in my life."

Everyone was thankful that Tara had brought two pizzas because Frank ate, ate, and then ate a little more.

Once full, the group sat back under the stars and enjoyed a beer.

"So," Tara said, "Are you up for another adventure?"

Frank assumed she was joking and laughed.

"I'm serious," Tara said. "I'm heading over to the island tomorrow. First, I'll be flying a helicopter to Victoria. Then, the plan is to spend a couple of days of sailing. Max says you were an avid sailor and taught him everything he knows."

Frank looked at Max. Was Tara serious?

Max shrugged. "Already charming, my fiancée, I see," he joked. "But seriously, I have to do some work in the next couple of days. So, you should go and enjoy yourself."

Frank thought about it. It was absurd. He had only met this young woman yesterday. He didn't want to be a burden. He had already had a big adventure. Did he need helicopter rides and sailing in the ocean? He had come all the way here to visit with his grandson. He couldn't be taking off to another part of the province.

Perhaps, another time, Frank thought.

But then, three little words came to Frank.

Why not now?

Chapter 10 Discussion Questions

1. Sometimes, we do things, big or small, where we even surprise ourselves. When is a time you have surprised yourself?

_____
_____
_____
_____

2. What kind of pizza is your favorite?

_____

3. Should Frank take Tara up on her offer for another adventure?

_____

4. Have you ever been in a helicopter?

_____

5. Have you ever been on a boat? If so, what kind of boats have you been on?

_____

_____

6. In your imagination, what would it be like if Frank decided to go on the adventure with Tara?

_____

_____

_____

_____

_____

_____

www.ingramcontent.com/pod-product-compliance
Lightning Source LLC
Chambersburg PA
CBHW070334120526
44590CB00017B/2883